The Poor Is The Rich

Financial Freedom for the Financially Literate

Jeremiah Jean-Bon

Jeremiah Jean-Bon

ISBN: 978-1-7372215-0-0

DEDICATION

This book is for the living generation.

CONTENTS

Jeremiah Jean-Bon

DISCLAIMER

I am a regular individual who looks for high-growth opportunities in the market. I want to prove that the average joe can gain financial freedom by obtaining the knowledge and skills needed for success, for those individuals to apply what they learn in their lifestyles.

Please do your own (DD) due diligence (research) and make sure to consult with your financial advisor before making any financial decisions. I am not a financial advisor; I am just a regular individual speaking out his thoughts and experiences.

SPEECH

Hello, my name is Jeremiah, and I am a college student! I wrote this book to inspire at least one person to be moved and motivate them to be greater than who they are today. Whether you are in a third-world country or a paradise, you can become financially free in this mindless world ruled by false teachings.

I wish that our school system can teach financial literacy to the students. It pains me to see how there can be people so cruel who have the power to change the internal problems they have in their country. They let the weak become weaker, and the strong become stronger. The strong prey on the weak, and the weak unknowingly let it stay as a norm.

As a person who is a nobody under the strong, I strive to become what others deem improbable. I will become financially free, worry-free in this lifetime. To be economically complimentary is to live life without worrying about not having money to pay for my expenses. I will not have to go to work if need not. I can be the one to give others, to be the giver. In this money-driven world, I will not recreate the wheel. I will follow those who left legacies, diaries, and any information imparted for the living generation.

To those still standing today, at the top, who gave their insight to help those below you, I thank you. Without any of you, I will not be writing this book. To those who inspired me and gave me the mental and spiritual strength to conquer my fears and to step into the dark knowledge of the richest, I thank you.

I am shedding tears writing this; my tears fill up my keyboard. It is not because of the knowledge I receive through my persistent hunger for knowledge of the rich. It is because of those who lack the knowledge and to those who do nothing with the knowledge.

I wish the broken world driven by greed, the inspiration from this book, will let their minds become free. To allow them to become whatever and whoever they want to be. Because life is meaningless without the hunger to enjoy, I will not let others judge me, ridicule me, and put me down because of my thirst for knowledge. I will continue to strive, learn, implement, and discipline myself on the path to success.

Success to me means that I have tried. Even if I die before reaching my goals, that is fine. I say that because I have something to show for it. I did not sit around and do nothing. Yet, I work hard to get where I want to be, and that, my friends, is the greatest testament that anyone on the path to financial freedom can state. When I die, I hope to leave a legacy, a new dream for those in the living generation. So that the living generation can look back and say, “I thank you.”

Welcome to my Book. The Poor is the Rich!

INTRO

I have always wondered why some people believe that human's lives are made predetermined by a higher entity. This entity chooses where we are born, our personality, and how our life will turn out to be. This belief is birth from the idea that very few people are born with a gold spoon, and others are born with a silver spoon or no spoon at all.

Many people would say that this is true. Some would say, "millionaires are born with a gold spoon in their mouths. That is how they stay rich! They pass their wealth to the next generation."

Well, sometimes I have asked those same people. "Have you ever seen a millionaire before?" Some would say yes; others would be lying. "Then if you haven't seen a millionaire, why make such assumptions?" The truth blinds some people, and delusions blind others. Where they get, their information could be from an unreliable source. Or their beliefs can be misguided because they are not educated about financial literacy.

Our public school system has not taught financial literacy to the students.

We are led to believe that students are to stay in school, learn what they can, and go to college to find a good well-paying job. It is like we cannot express ourselves or refrain from moving out of the cycle to obey orders. Not to be the one who gives orders.

We are not taught what a credit card is, what is a mortgage, what is auto insurance? There is a lack of education that we lack in the school system. Many people struggle to live paycheck to paycheck because they were not taught how to use their money wisely.

Of course, I can blame the school system, but it is not entirely their fault. We, the people, need to put in the efforts to learn about such things. Without the desire to learn, where can our wisdom lead us?

As a college student living in Florida, the United States of America, I am writing this book to share my beliefs, ideals, and perspective on society.

I wish that everyone can become financially responsible for themselves and stop blaming others for the situation that they find themselves in.

I wish everyone could realize that you are not destined only to be where you Think you are meant to be. It is what you make out of your situation to something new; you can make your financial situation much better.

But before we can do that, we must understand this dilemma first. The problem is that "The Poor Is the Rich."

THE POOR BECOMES POORER

When you are shopping in a store with a child, the child finds a toy or candy that he or she wants, ends up asking you if you can buy it for them. As a parent, you might contemplate whether you should buy it for them. There are only two choices: either you give in to what they want or say no and end up hearing them crying and whining until your drive home.

However, asked yourself this? Is the item the child is asking for is a need, or is it a want? That is imperative to understand the difference between what is necessary and what is not. That is very relatable to how individuals view the things that they purchase.

A need is what is essential to one's life. A want is a desire to have something but could live without it.

There is an essential difference between the two. Yet why do people make it harder than it seems to understand? Is it because they genuinely do not care, or they choose to get what they want? Is it because they are providing excuses to fill them with doubt? What do you believe could be the answer?

Whatever answer it could be, this does not change the fact that most people cannot differentiate between a need and a want. They choose to do what their hearts pull them to do, and then they wonder why they are financially unstable.
The poor cannot discipline themselves and are not willing to change their lifestyles for the better. Have a look around you, and you will see what I am seeing.

Credit Cards/Credit Score

Americans have tried to use the idea of credit cards are good for you. Building your credit score is needed in building wealth. We need to get in debt to get in control of the money we do not own. I have heard individuals say that "I need to get a mortgage to own a home, and then I would use the appreciated equity to buy another home to grow my wealth. I will continue with this process over the next few years."

Using an idea like that blows my mind. Buying homes with equity in repetition as long the bank gives me a mortgage. Buying may seem like a great idea in a bull market, but have you ever seen what had happened in the 2008/2009 recession. Many people over-leverage in the homes that they do not 'own.' Most of those people who were full of debt ended falling into foreclosure.

So, I say these things because, in most states, you will never truly own the properties you've purchase. It will not matter if you have a mortgage or paid your home in cash. The government owns your home. Imagine if you never pay your property tax; what would happen? A tax lien ends up being a mark against your home, and if you fail to pay the taxes, the tax collector will have to sell your home eventually. Afterward, you would be homeless.

Undoubtedly, most people would instead build up debt than being debt-free. People are scared to stop using credit and borrowing debt because they do not want to lose their credit score. A credit score only shows how much you love debt and how you manage debt, not how you manage your money. That is why I say stop being foolish and grow out of the mindset that a credit score is beneficial for you because it is not.

I have heard others say that 'you are losing more money using a debit card and gain more with the cashback of a credit card.' I genuinely say that some people are foolish because they unknowingly believe cashback is excellent as an incentive to use credit cards. Cashback is a tactic from credit companies and financial institutions to draw in more users for their products. You will only gain cashback from the things you spend on. Meaning the more you spend, the more cashback you will get. These companies are so innovative because they know what they are doing. They are willing to pay more so that you can make monthly payments with interest as high as 24.99% or more. So, who is genuinely winning, is it you or is the issuer of the credit cards?

Financing- Lease & Loan Part 1

I remember when I was younger each year, a new iPhone would come out in September. The hype that everyone is dying to have a repeat of the same 'new' iPhone blows my intelligence away. When I was younger, I have seen adults around me would try to get their hands on the new iPhone. I have never understood the reason or the desire to have the latest edition even until now, yet they seem like they always have the money to buy a new phone knowing that we are broke. It was until I grew older and learned of the money mugging tool of financing.

The dark tool of financing allows individuals who do not have enough funds to purchase a phone to finance their phone using a lease or a loan. Some individuals use the loan option to buy their phones. With a loan, an individual would have a monthly installment plan. In this contract, the purchaser will 'own' the phone when they have finished paying at the end of their term.

With the lease option, poor people can rent a phone. The individual would have to pay a monthly payment, and they would not 'own' the phone. However, they may choose to buy the remaining balance for the phone if they choose to accept it outright.

These two financing choices give poor people the ability to buy something that they cannot afford. The telecommunication companies are so innovative and using tactics to keep people in a loop. And better yet, poor people have a choice of using 'Early Upgrade.' With this, an individual can upgrade to a new phone at no extra cost to them. This choice increases the duration of the contracts, and the monthly payments will increase.

With this, telecommunication companies use these contracts to keep their customers locked in cages, which allows the customers to feel like they did the right thing getting into such agreements. This is how they felt. Poor people do not see the bigger picture; they only see what is in front of them.

Financing- Lease & Loan Part 2

I love how these same tactics are used in the auto industry. Besides a mortgage, a car payment is the second most significant problem that drives people away from the path to financial freedom. Again, there are two ways to finance your car. It is through a lease or a loan.

A lease allows you to pay to use the car, but it does not allow you to pay for the vehicle itself. Meaning you do not obtain any ownership of the car. Usually, you will be making fewer monthly payments and paying a money factor-like interest rate. The massive downside with a lease is that you will not inherit any equity in the vehicle to trade in. Regardless, the equity in the car will not amount to much because the longer you have the vehicle, the more value you remove out of it.

Another downside with a lease is that you would have to make sure you are within the specified miles of use. Auto Companies or dealerships love to charge people for mile penalty. Which in turn also charge the customer for wear and tear when the car is not appropriately maintained.

When it comes to a loan, you are paying monthly, and the payment is usually higher than a lease because you are 'buying the car. With this plan, you can use the equity you have to trade in with another vehicle. Some people use this tactic to get a new car and keep themselves in a loop. Meaning they are continuing to be in debt with this cycle. In the meantime, you are still buying a depreciating asset, and it will continue to lose value throughout the car until the car is unusable.

Working for Money

Have you heard the phrase, 'the poor works for money, the middle-class saves, and the rich invests?' This phrase applies in our society.

Most people in America are living paycheck to paycheck. Some people have no clue how they will get by for the next day; others have a clue knowing that their entire paycheck is going straight into expenses. There is no money left for investing, and better yet, there is no money in the emergency fund.

Why are most of these problems are towards the poor? This is because they have the mindset is to work to make a living. Most people are scared that they may get fired or lose a raise because of fear. The poor believe that having a career gives you job security, which is not valid! If you work for someone else, you are always replaceable!

Why do poor people feel this way?

Poor people do not know how to make money outside of their jobs. In this sense, while you are working for someone else, you do not have any control, which means you cannot determine how much money to pay yourself or when you should come to work. It is all up to the hand of your employer.

THE RICH BECOMES RICHER

There is a notion that millionaires became who they are because their parents gave them money. Again, this money became theirs because they were lucky. They were fated to be given a golden spoon. This is something that the working class can never achieve, even in their wildest dreams!

Well, I am here to tell those who believe that is very wrong. I cannot wrap my head around how people think something they have never verified to see if this is real. It is like saying out of all the millionaires I have met; there were all heirs to their predecessors. So, they were able to receive this lump sum of money like they have won the lottery.

Have you taken the time to read a book that details how many millionaires became who they are today? Or if not, why do you not google how many millionaires are self-made? The information is out there; it is not hiding from you! It is not a top-secret that anyone cannot get access to.

Most millionaires today are self-made! Most of them are self-made! I said this twice to emphasize the importance of this! They were not rich beforehand, so they were either in the middle class or in the poor class.
Now after finding out that most millionaires were not handed golden eggs. What should you ask yourself?

Here are two questions you should ask yourself:

What are they doing differently from me that they were able to reach this status?

What should I do to become financially free?

Well, let us investigate the mind of rich people to see how they invest their money.

Income Producing Assets

Where do you place your money? Is it a new car, a new phone, or a piece of contemporary furniture? Which is it? Do you put your money into something because it is something that you desire? Is this a need or a want?

The rich places the money into income-producing assets. This means the rich invest in things with value that increases over time. Each buy is a calculated buy. Relative questions they could ask themselves is: Will this asset fit in my budget for purchase? What will be my expected rate of return will be? Am I buying this because of emotional attachment?

Most of a rich individual net worth is in income-producing assets. The rich do not carry most of their money in cash; it is usually tied up in assets. Investments that increase in value over time. It can be in the form of real estate, stocks, bonds, or their own business.
The rich know what should be done so they can keep their status. So, they may pass on their wealth from one generation to the next. They have the knowledge, and they act on it with repetition. The wealthy stay wealthy and become richer over time.

Willing to Learn.

Schooling has been something that I hate, and others can account for this. Some say college is not for them. They will not be able to learn anything while being in school! Why is that?

Some people are not able to sit in front of a classroom listening to a lecture. Others are not able to comprehend the instructions and assignments given to them. They feel like school is a waste of time. Why is that?
You can say the material they are learning in school does not relate to them, or they must be lazy. They must be illiterate if they cannot sit down in class for few hours. Why is that?

It is not because of these options above. It is because the school does not talk about what is essential. The most important in life is how to manage your money. It is to become financially literate, and this is what the rich yearn!
The rich are willing to gain knowledge. Continuous learning is the key to becoming wealthy. From making mistakes to correcting them and making

decisions on a larger scale, they succeed in the end. They are willing to sacrifice the traditional path of the poor they so-called success and become much more significant than that.

The rich involve themselves around knowledge and skills that are important. Skills and expertise concerning investing, budgeting, taxes/accounting, and self-discipline themselves act with money.

Control

The Rich was able to create something that they have control over. When you are working for another person, they have control over you. The rich do not want to be in a situation where they can be replaced. Instead of waiting to be replaced, they work their way to be the ones replacing people. This is through starting your own business.

A side hustle that can turn into a long-term income-producing business. That can be a way for individuals to multiply their income by many times. This is because the rich are in control. Being in power allows you to determine every step that you should take in your business.

Working a traditional job will be hard to multiply your income on a fast and efficient scale. There is a limit to how someone can make by working for others. The rich know this, and they figure out ways for them to start.

It is better to fail many times and learn from it and continue to try to make it. Then having the knowledge and have never started anything. The rich will continue to try and implement changes to improve from their previous failures.

When you have your own business, it is only the individual who limits themselves. Being under someone else has a cap. But the one who starts their own business has the control to scale up however much they want to achieve success.

Money work for them

The rich save so much money from taxes in the act of passive income. Passive income is the money that is made from assets or investments that produce income for the individual with no effort. The rich make their money from passive income, and the poor make their money from active income. Active income is the money that is earned from performing a service, such as wages, salaries, tips, commission, etc.

The rich did not participate in such things. They created wealth so that their wealth can produce more income for them. Their money can make an income while they are sleeping, pooping, and eating.

Some people can ask themselves how the rich can achieve this. The rich can accomplish this through investments. Real estate is one form of passive income the rich can obtain. They own homes, condos, business buildings, and other real estate assets. They can rent them to receive monthly payments through a lease or a contract.

Another form of passive income, which is, in my opinion, is the purest is dividends. Dividends are profits given to shareholders of a stock. The companies are paying you to hold shares of a company with no effort at all.

The rich use this tactic to receive passive income. They can receive payments every month, every quarter, every six months, or every year.

There are just two primary examples of many other tactics the rich use to gain passive income.

Taxes

Every year it is very imperative to fill your 1040 form with a W-2 form. Also, to pay taxes to the government. Why is this important? So that you may be free from the gazes of Uncle Sam. And yet, sometimes we hear that rich people pay no taxes. Why is that?

Have you ever heard the name, Warren Buffett? He is the CEO of Berkshire Hathaway, with a net worth of about $100 Billion. He said that he pays fewer taxes than his secretary. A person who is a billionaire who pays fewer taxes than someone who is not even in the same realm of income does not make any sense.
This is because the rich understand the tax code. It is by no means that Warren Buffett pays fewer taxes. It is by the percentage of which he pays is less than his secretary. He knows how to use the tax system to his advantage. The rich know how to use the tax system to their advantage.

In the world of the rich, there is a saying that applies to their hearts. It is about how much you make, how much you keep from the tax system, and how much you pass on to your next generation! [How much you make, how much you keep, and how much you pass on]

The rich know how to hide behind legal entities such as an S Corp, LLC, and corporations, etc. The rich know how to use non-for-profit charity organizations to their advantage. So that they can hide their money within a system that will benefit themselves, which is legal through the tax system.

Another example we can use is the Ex-president of the united states, Donald Trump. There was a period in the year 2020 where the American people (poor people) did not understand how Donald Trump paid only 750 dollars in 2017. In 10 years of the 15 years previously, he paid no taxes to the government. The American people wanted Donald Trump to show his tax documents to the world.

At first, it is none of our business about the information of his taxes. I am not pro-trump, but would you like to have others looking into your personal tax information intensively? The rich already knew why he only paid 750 dollars in taxes, and yet the poor did not.

This is because you can carry your losses from the previous year's forward and write them off your future gains in a corporate structure. There have been many other people and companies that did the same things as Donald did. For instance, Amazon, a vast digital marketplace for people to shop, has paid no taxes to the U.S. government for many years. Again, this is because they understood the tax code and wrote off their previous losses against their gains.

There are many ways to use the tax system to your advantage. The only way to learn how is to do your research or find an expert who is knowledgeable in the field of taxes, just like the rich.

The Poor is The Rich

OUTRO

Unlike all things, I have said in this book. I understand that not every poor person acts like the rich, and not every rich person acts like the poor.

For the rich to act like the poor is very subjective. Some wealthy individuals spent their money like there is no tomorrow. Others spend their money as they must live for an eternity.

However, if you are in a position or in a country that gives opportunities, take it. If you cannot find opportunities, create them. There is no excuse for you to live your life that you and others believe to be predetermined.

Of course, not everyone will find the path to success. Most people are not going to find their meaning in life along with chasing money. There will always be a need to have a working class. Every person cannot be the person giving orders. There will always be someone to do the work that others do not want to do in this world where many people do not have the will to do more than what seems to be destined for them. There is an opportunity for those who have the knowledge and the choice to do more to become the person they are willing to be.

If you are willing to crawl out of the life that may seem destined for you. There are a few things that you can do.

Learn.

Apply.

Discipline.

Repeat.

Gain the knowledge needed for the start of your journey. Apply the knowledge to your lifestyle and discipline yourself on the path to success. And repeat the steps. You will never stop learning. There is an endless amount of information waiting for you. You will continue to find the knowledge and search for the people who know and be willing to teach you. You will continue to improve your craft. Whether you are starting a business, investing, moving up a corporate ladder, or whatever you must do to achieve your success, you will continue to improve to be better and become closer to your goals.

I know that many people in situations that may seem out of their control. Some people are struggling to try to make rent payments, working an 80-hour week to make sure their kids have food on the table. People in 3rd world countries who do not even have electricity or clean water are trying to make it day by day.

For those who were able to read this book, I want to say you are not alone with these feelings and many people feel your pain. I want to tell you, do not Give up! I want you to strive to become whatever or whoever you desire. Do not let anything hold you back. There is no entity holding you back; no destiny or fate is holding you back. There is only one person that can hold you back, and that person is yourself. It would only be you doing so. So, stay strong and work hard to get where you want to be!

Find your passion, along with chasing your goals. Pursue meaning along the path to financial success.

Mindset

At the end of each day, it is all about the mindset. Financial education is not about working for money. It is all about how I can allow money to work for me.

You can say that going to school and getting a high-paying job is the way to go because this is what you have been taught. Most people come out of school with student loan debt or may come out with a degree but still do not know anything about money. Graduates may have jobs, but the jobs may go away. How can one secure income with only one income source?

The person with a poor mindset who falls would not know how to get up. But the person with a decadent attitude would say thank you for letting me fall so that I can get up and run faster than before.

Sometimes in life, you may have to do something you hate to get to where you want to be. Working a 9-5 job, cutting grass, or working at the city dump, can allow you to have money to invest in the things you love. It is not about passion but the purpose of driving you to what you love.

Learning about the stock market, or reading books, learn about taxes, and such. Things that people will hate to do. You must be mentally ready to understand what the rich know, and by doing so, you are willing to give your time to learn them. Remember, give a man a fish, and you feed him for a day; teach a man to fish, and you feed him for a lifetime. Time is your greatest asset!

It is you who must gain the knowledge and be willing to learn. Open your mind to the wealthy mindset and get rid of the poor attitude and let your mind soar. You will have to do what you hate first to drive you to the path to do what you want. Whether it takes years to reach your goals because, in the end, the thing you would love the most is your freedom. Doing so will allow you to be financially free to do whatever your heart desire. However, this all starts with the mindset.

ABOUT THE AUTHOR

Hello!

My name is Jeremiah Jean-Bon.

I am a high-growth investor and a college student who loves talking about the realm of investing.

It took me many years to gain the knowledge needed to invest. Over time while trying different aspects of investing, I overcame a lot of challenges and unknowns. Yet, it made me who I am today.

I am willing to share what I learn and committed to helping others to the road to financial freedom and allow them to become finically literate.

Sharing my knowledge is my passion, and I hope you and I can grow while chasing our goals.

Made in the USA
Monee, IL
04 November 2026

67374664R00020